THE ROMANS
IN SCOTLAND

**An introduction to the collections of the
National Museum of Antiquities of Scotland**

D V Clarke, D J Breeze & Ghillean Mackay

National Museum of Antiquities of Scotland

Edinburgh 1980

Front cover:
Marble head from Hawkshaw, Tweedsmuir, Peeblesshire. It
has been suggested that this extremely well carved head once
formed part of a triumphal monument erected in the
Lowlands of Scotland to commemorate the Roman conquest
of the area. It dates to the early years of the 2nd century AD.

ISBN 0 11 491637 3

CONTENTS

INTRODUCTION

David J Breeze

The Roman army controlled southern Scotland for nearly 3 centuries from AD 80 when Agricola first conquered the Lowland tribes, until 367, when, following a concerted attack by her barbarian enemies, Rome seems to have lost or given up control of this area. Roman troops were stationed in strength in Scotland for only two short periods, each of about twenty years, at the end of the first century and in the middle of the second, but for the rest of these centuries control was exercised by troops based in forts on, or just behind, the present Anglo-Scottish border. The years when southern Scotland was part of the Roman Empire had little effect on her history yet the Romans have left vivid traces of their presence in the form of earthworks and artifacts. This booklet is essentially concerned with the latter, but in order to be able to understand their importance it is essential to place them in their wider setting.

The first definite Roman contact with Scotland was in AD 80. In that year the governor of the province of Britain, Gnaeus Julius Agricola, acting on the instructions of the Emperor Titus, advanced through the Scottish lowlands and reconnoitred as far north as the River Tay. The tribes of southern Scotland were incorporated into the province, forts were established on the Forth-Clyde line and the possibility of creating a permanent frontier on this line was considered. However, the accession of the Emperor Domitian in 81 led to a resumption of the advance, Agricola attacking and, in 84, defeating the Highland tribes. The site of his famous victory, Mons Graupius, is not known, but probably lay north of the Mounth in Aberdeenshire. Agricola, after an unusually long 7 year governorship, was replaced and it was left to his successor to organise the construction of forts in the newly conquered area.

Before this process was completed Roman reverses on the Danube frontier led to troop withdrawals from Britain and an abandonment of the northern forts in Strathearn and Strathmore. The re-adjustment of Roman forces in north Britain appears to have taken place in two stages. At first the outer line of forts along the edge of the Highlands, including the legionary fortress at Inchtuthil, was abandoned while still under construction and a new frontier was established in the centre of Strathmore. Then this frontier was abandoned and with it the forts in the Forth valley and Clydesdale. From about 90 to 105 the most northerly forts in the province lay just north of the Cheviots on a line from Newstead in Tweeddale to Glenlochar beside Castle Douglas in Kirkcudbright. About 105 there were further troop reductions in north Britain, presumably again in connection with warfare on the Danube, and as a result all the remaining forts north of the Tyne-Solway isthmus were abandoned. In the 120s the Emperor Hadrian ordered the construction of a new frontier, Hadrian's Wall, on this line.

The frontier complex created by Hadrian was abandoned by his successor, Antoninus Pius, who ordered the re-occupation of southern

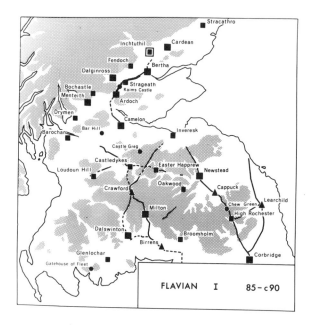

FLAVIAN I 85 – c90

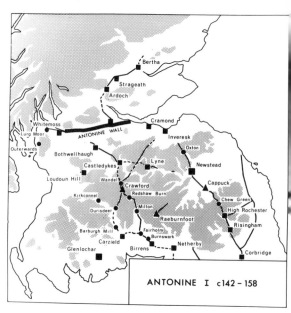

ANTONINE I c142 – 158

Scotland and the construction of a new wall across the Forth-Clyde isthmus. The reasons for this change in policy are unclear but may be connected with Pius's own problems in Rome rather than any supposed frontier disturbance in Britain: Pius may have felt the need to strengthen his position by gaining the prestige of fighting a successful war and extending the boundary of the empire. There were modifications to the original troop dispositions during Pius's reign, perhaps even a move to return to Hadrian's Wall, quashed probably by Pius himself. Pius's conquests, however, lasted little longer than his reign for shortly after his death in 161 his successors, the Emperors Marcus and Verus, abandoned the Antonine Wall and most of the forts in Scotland and restored Hadrian's Wall.

The system of frontier control established in the 160s was to last for 200 years with minor changes and but one interlude. Outpost forts were established to the north of Hadrian's Wall. At first these outposts extended as far north as Newstead on the Tweed, and possibly even included Castlecary on the now abandoned Antonine Wall, and as far west as Birrens in Dumfriesshire, but by the early years of the third century the furthermost forts had been abandoned leaving four forts which were occupied until the second half of the fourth century. These forts were the bases for large, mobile auxiliary units and also scouts, together

capable of wide ranging patrolling and of withstanding all but the most serious attack. It has been suggested that these troops supervised the eight tribal *loca*, generally interpreted as meeting places or markets, in the area between Hadrian's Wall and the Tay.

Within forty years of the abandonment of the Antonine Wall the northern barbarians twice invaded the province and in 208 the seriousness of the situation caused the Emperor Septimius Severus to come to Britain to lead the Roman counter-attack. The barbarians were defeated, though not without difficulty, and ceded territory to Rome. A new legionary base was established at Carpow on the Tay, apparently to be the focus for the new occupation of Scotland. However, the death of Severus at York in 211 led to the abandonment of his plans, and with them Carpow.

The northern frontier in the following years appears to have been peaceful, but the end of the third century saw the first reference to a new nation, the Picts, an amalgamation of earlier tribes in Scotland, and a changing political situation. The hostile attitude of the Picts led to campaigns against them by the Emperor Constantius in 305, possibly by the Emperor Constantine in 314, and, it would appear, to serious trouble which demanded the presence of the Emperor Constans in Britain in the winter of

342/3. In the 360s the Picts combined with other peoples, Scots, Saxons, Franks and Attacotti, to attack the Romans and after the most serious invasion in 367 Rome appears to have lost control over the territory north of Hadrian's Wall. Sporadic warfare continued into the fifth century but the Roman occupation of southern Scotland can be said to have ended in 367, nearly 300 years after Agricola had conquered the Lowland tribes and reached the Tay.

In many ways these 300 years are an interlude in the later prehistoric period in Scotland, but the presence of the Roman army did have an effect on the people of the time. In AD 80 most people in south Scotland lived in round timber huts, sometimes grouped together to form villages. Often these homesteads and settlements were defended by earthen banks and ditches. Some of these defended settlements or forts were so large that they have been interpreted as tribal capitals. One such fort is on Eildon Hill North where about 300 hut platforms have been recognised within a triple series of ramparts and ditches: the population may have been about 2,000. These people kept sheep and cattle and also probably grew some cereals. Their diet would have been supplemented by hunting, fishing and collecting wild food.

The Roman army imposed peace. Fort defences were abandoned, presumably at the behest of the army, and in time houses were built over the crumbling ramparts. These houses were often of stone in eastern Scotland, though in the west timber continued to be the main material used. Peace also, it appears, brought an increase in population. Existing settlements were extended and new ones established by groups leaving their ancestral homes. Another factor leading to the growth of the agricultural community will have been the presence of the Roman troops in Scotland. The army needed food, leather, wool for clothing and, as far as possible, will have obtained these supplies locally. Other local resources such as minerals, and recruits, may have been tapped, though no evidence of this survives.

The presence of the army brought about another change in the distribution of the local population. The good pay of the Roman soldiers attracted civilians to forts to help the soldiers spend their money. Civil settlements probably grew up beside most Roman forts in Scotland, though little is known of them. One such site on the Antonine Wall, the village at Carriden by Bo'ness, was awarded self-governing rights. The shops, taverns, inns and brothels built by civilians would have been supplemented by temples, most probably built by soldiers. Soldiers will also have built houses for their families—they were not allowed to marry but many contracted unofficial unions with local women—and no doubt retired there on completion of their army service. The Romans were not in Scotland long enough to allow these settlements to establish themselves and following the Roman withdrawal they seem to have died.

If the Roman peace and the Roman army brought some tangible benefits to the local inhabitants, little evidence of their material prosperity survives. There was a "drift" of artifacts—brooches, pottery, glass—from the Roman province to the tribes beyond the frontier, but on the whole there is little to show for the 300 years contact between Rome and the northern tribes. Roman artifacts did reach the settlements of southern Scotland, but in very small quantities. Some finds travelled further afield for Roman objects have been found as far north as Shetland and as far west as Lewis, but the distribution suggests coastal trade, possibly even plunder, though there is no specific evidence of this.

If there is no evidence for plunder, there is a hint at the payment of subsidies by the Romans to the tribes beyond the frontier. The discovery of coin hoards in southern Scotland in the late second and early third centuries may give support to the words of contemporary writers who imply the use of this branch of diplomacy on the northern frontier.

The payment of subsidies was, however, only one weapon at Rome's disposal. The explicit expression of Rome's power was the fort and the troops based there—the Roman army, the legions and the auxiliary units. The legions were composed of Roman citizens, though by the late first century AD those in the western half of the Empire were mainly recruited from provinces outside Italy such as France and Spain. The auxiliaries, originally a mixture of contingents from friends of Rome, provincial levies and mercenaries, by the late first century AD were generally recruited from frontier provinces. Local recruiting became increasingly more usual for both legions and auxiliary units so that by the early third century most of the units based in Britain were formed mainly of men from the island. The Roman army was for the most part a volunteer army—conscription was rarely resorted to—and both legionaries and auxiliaries served for 25 years.

The legions formed the back-bone of the Roman army. Each contained just over 5,000 well-armed highly disciplined men trained to fight set-piece battles. The legionaries were not just soldiers but were skilled in other crafts such as building and engineering. There were usually only three legions based in Britain and none was ever permanently stationed in Scotland though detachments from the legions helped garrison forts in Scotland.

The rough and tumble of frontier warfare in north Britain and most of the garrison duties were undertaken by the auxiliary units. Auxiliaries were not normally Roman citizens, but received citizenship, a prized privilege, on their retirement. These soldiers were usually protected by mail shirts and iron helmets and carried swords and spears. They were organised into units, formed of infantry or cavalry or a combination of both, either 500 or 1,000 strong.

In the late first century and in the middle of the second century when Roman forces occupied southern Scotland up to the Tay the tribes of the area were controlled by a network of forts and fortlets connected by roads. In the main river valleys were placed large forts: an example is Newstead in Tweeddale. Some of these were large enough to have held more than a single auxiliary unit and may have had mixed garrisons of legionaries and auxiliaries. Between these large forts lay smaller forts each capable of holding a single auxiliary unit and in certain areas there were placed even smaller stations or fortlets. The fortlet, usually garrisoned by 80 men or less, was particularly common in south-west Scotland in the mid-second century.

Although in the late first century the construction of a legionary fortress at Inchtuthil was commenced the work was not completed and the site was abandoned unfinished. In the early third century the Emperor Septimius Severus constructed a legionary base at Carpow on the Tay but this also was abandoned within a few years of its construction.

In the years following the arrival of Roman forces in Britain in AD 43 there was no strongly defended frontier line to the province. However, when in the 80s Rome for the first time consciously considered rejecting the idea of conquering the whole island of Britain, a frontier was established across the Forth-Clyde isthmus. This was of short duration as the Roman army continued its northern advance a couple of years later. The gains of these years, which should have been consolidated by the occupation of the Highlands, were never realised and in the late 80s a frontier, the first real frontier in Britain and among the first anywhere in the empire, was constructed utilising the Gask Ridge in Strathmore for part of its length. Here the existing line of forts was supplemented by the construction of watch-towers. The function of the soldiers stationed here was to keep watch or a cleared strip of ground and control the movement of people in and out of the province. There was no linear barrier or wall and this element was not added to frontier systems for another 30 years or more, long after the abandonment of the Gask frontier.

The Antonine Wall, built in the light of experience gained on Hadrian's Wall, was constructed in the years following the Roman reoccupation of Scotland in 140–142. In its completed form it consisted of a turf rampart, at least 10 feet high, on a stone base, 15 Roman feet wide. In front of the rampart lay a wide and deep ditch and the material from this was tipped out on the north lip to form a glacis or outer mound. Behind the rampart ran a road, the Military Way. This road connected the forts on the Wall which were usually placed at intervals of about 2 miles along its whole length. Between certain forts have been found fortlets and it seems probable that there was originally a fort or fortlet at every mile interval. In some areas other small enclosures are known while three pairs of

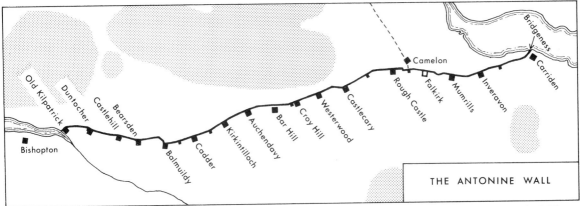

Solid squares=known forts   open squares=presumed forts

Copyright D J Breeze

beacon platforms to aid in communication with forts in advance or to the rear of the Wall have also been discovered.

The existence of forts in front of the Wall demonstrates that this was not a frontier in the modern sense. The Wall was placed in the most convenient geographical position and its purpose was, like the forts and watch-towers on the Gask frontier, to monitor the movement of people into and out of the province. The Wall, and the troops based there, would prevent petty raiding and thus allow the peaceful economic exploitation of the Wall's hinterland, but they would not necessarily prevent a large scale attack on the frontier. Such an attack would in any case be countered by the army in the field, not from behind earth ramparts.

In order to prepare for such fighting the Roman army spent a considerable amount of time training and on manoeuvres. Two training grounds exist in Scotland, at Burnswark in Dumfriesshire and at Woden Law in Roxburghshire. Indeed the last place we would find Roman soldiers in summer would be in their forts.

The Roman fort was a compact collection of buildings serving the needs of the unit(s) based there. Surrounded by a stone wall or earth rampart and at least two ditches were a headquarters building, house for the commanding officer, granaries, barrack-blocks, stables and storehouses. In the first century the buildings were usually all of timber, but thereafter frequently the principal buildings

were of stone, or at least timber on stone sill-walls, and the barracks, stables, etc of timber. There were no communal messing facilities in the Roman army: each soldier, or group of soldiers, was supplied with his own rations and cooked them in hearths or ovens usually placed immediately inside the rampart. Great care was taken over hygiene. Most units had their own doctor(s) and all forts had latrines (usually apparently flushed by water) and a bath-house provided for the use of all the men in the unit.

Although Scotland was on the far north-west frontier of Rome and was but briefly part of the Roman empire, traces of the Roman occupation are particularly well-preserved. The range and quality of surviving earthworks, earthworks which were once camps, fortresses, forts, fortlets, watch-towers, signal-stations, training areas or frontiers and the roads which formerly linked them, is perhaps greater in Scotland than in any other country and there exists in Scotland's museums some remarkable artifacts which help clothe these earthworks. The visitor to Roman Scotland and this museum is singularly fortunate in the state of the remains which survive to recall a civilisation which flourished about 2,000 years ago.

CATALOGUE

D V Clarke & Ghillean Mackay

The final two entries give the Museum's catalogue number and wherever appropriate a reference for each object or group of objects. The reference takes the form of the author, year and page only at the end of each catalogue entry with full details in the list of references at the end of the catalogue.

The following abbreviations have been used:

D   diameter
H   height
L   length
W   width

All measurements are given in metres (m) or millimetres (mm).

We should like to thank Mr I L Scott without whose continual help this catalogue would have taken much longer to prepare. We should also like to thank Dr J Close-Brooks, Mrs H Bennett, Mr I F Larner, who took the photographs, Miss Helen Jackson who prepared the line drawings, Mr Charles J Burnett, and Miss Linda Morris. For help with photographs, we thank The Scotsman, the Royal Bank of Scotland (Princes Street Branch), the Scottish Development Department, Ancient Monuments, J H Rogers & Co Ltd, Saddlers, and J H Bonnar, Jeweller.

I THE ANTONINE WALL

The ditch of the Antonine Wall at Watling Lodge.
Photograph: Scottish Development Department, Ancient Monuments.

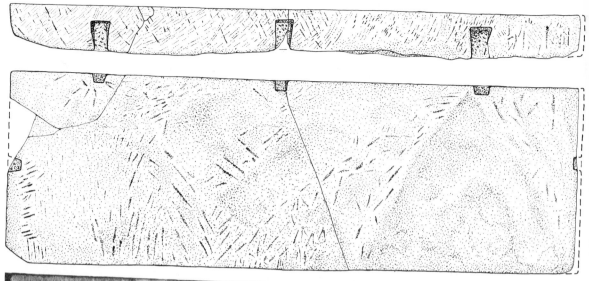

The drawings show the back and top edge of the slab where there are holes for metal clamps

1 Dedication-slab

Mid 2nd century AD
Bridgeness, West Lothian
L 2.74m

This slab, the most elaborate of any known from the Antonine Wall, was found at the east end of the Wall where it meets the Firth of Forth. The central inscription is flanked by two scenes. That on the left symbolises the Roman conquest and shows a Roman cavalryman riding over four naked Britons armed with swords and shields. One of the Britons is already beheaded and another has a spear shaft in his back. On the right is shown the *suovetaurilia*, a ceremony undertaken before important campaigns or in this case before the Wall was built. A bull, a sheep and a pig are waiting to be sacrificed. A musician is playing a double flute while a priest in a toga pours a libation on the altar watched by a group of soldiers one of whom holds a flag inscribed LEG II AVG (Second Legion Augusta).

The inscription reads as follows:

IMP(ERATORI) CAES(ARI) TITO AELIO
HADRI(ANO) ANTONINO
AVG(VSTO) PIO P(ATRI) P(ATRIAE) LEG(IO) II
AVG(VSTA) PER M(ILIA) P(ASSVVM) IIII
DCLII FEC(IT)

This may be translated as follows:
For the Emperor Caesar Titus Aelius
Hadrianus Antoninus Augustus Pius, father
of his country, the Second Legion Augusta
built (this work) for a distance of 4,652 paces.
The stone has five sockets for metal clamps cut in
its edges which suggests it was set in a stone
frame. On the front of the slab are traces of
original red paint, most easily seen in the incised
lettering and the ornamental peltas on each side
of the inscription, and on the cloak of the right-
hand soldier. The slab dates to
AD 142–3 when the Wall was built.

FV 27
*Collingwood & Wright 1965, 657–58, no 2139,
pl XVIII; Phillips 1974*

II THE SOLDIERS

The Kings Own Scottish Borderers (the Edinburgh Regiment)
c 1902; from the memorial on the North Bridge, Edinburgh.

2 The legionaries

2nd century AD
Croy Hill, Dumbartonshire—a Roman fort
on the Antonine Wall
H 370mm

This stone relief was probably part of a free-standing tombstone and shows three legionaries. The two figures on the left each hold a spear in the right hand and have their shields resting on the ground on the left. Their helmets hang over the top of the shields held by their chin-straps. The figure on the right also has a shield but he carries it on his left arm, as when in action, and in his right hand he holds a drawn sword. His helmet, presumably grasped in the fingers of his left hand, is visible in front of his body. All three are wearing a cloak, a cuirass and a tunic. They may be a father and two sons.

FV 43
*Macdonald 1934a, 446–47, pl 47.2; Toynbee
1964, 188*

3 Iron helmet

Late 1st century AD
Newstead, Roxburghshire—a Roman fort
H 150mm

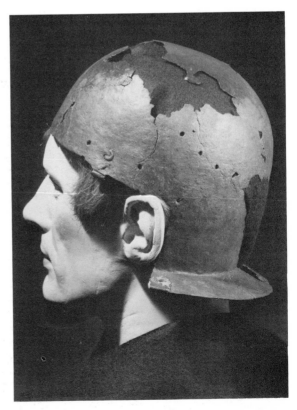

This example of an auxiliary cavalry helmet, although devoid of almost all its fittings, is still one of the best preserved examples known. It is very simple in form, covering the head and coming well down over the brow. At the back it is continued down into a deep neck-guard from the bottom of which is a projecting rim. The hinge plates for the cheekpieces survive and there are several holes on the helmet indicating further fittings, now missing. A small amount of silver sheathing is still preserved on the neck-guard.

FRA 124
Curle 1911, 164, pl XXVI; Robinson 1975, 95, pl 246

4 Armour fragments

Late 1st–2nd century AD
Newstead, Roxburghshire—a Roman fort
L (of the largest fragment) 215mm

Over forty fragments from a piece of body armour were found in the well in the headquarters building at Newstead. The armour was made in segments to provide the necessary flexibility. It is iron with brass fittings and was mounted on leather straps. The basic pattern involves a pair of three plates rivetted together which can be joined to protect the upper chest and back. Over these and held together by leather straps were a series of overlapping plates to protect the shoulder. A set of six overlapping girdle plates were hung by a hook and leather strap from the main plates.

FRA 117
Curle 1911, 156–58, pl XXII; Robinson 1975, 174–84, fig 181, pl 487–88

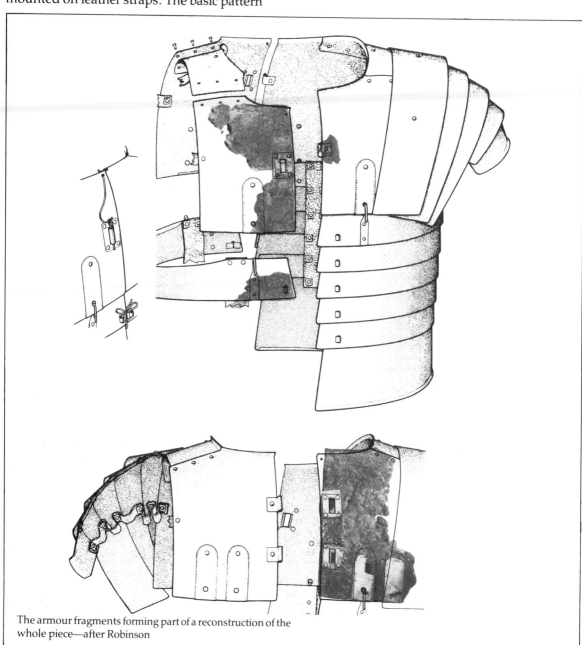

The armour fragments forming part of a reconstruction of the whole piece—after Robinson

5 Iron sword

Late 1st century AD
Newstead, Roxburghshire—a Roman fort
L 725mm

The blade of this long, narrow sword has a pronounced mid-rib giving a lozenge-shaped cross-section. There is a long tang on which would have fitted the handle of bone or wood. Swords of this type are generally interpreted as the weapons of the cavalry units.

FRA 134
Curle 1911, 183–84, pl XXXIV

6 Bronze chape

Late 1st—2nd century AD
Newstead, Roxburghshire—a Roman fort
W 60mm

The chape strengthened the bottom of the scabbard and needed to be made of metal to prevent the tip of the sword piercing it. The scabbard would be largely made of organic material, such as wood or leather, held together by bronze bindings.

FRA 153
Curle 1911, 187, pl XXXV

7 Iron arrowheads

2nd century AD
Newstead, Roxburghshire—a Roman fort
L (of the largest example) 50mm

These barbed and tanged arrowheads all have a characteristically fluted, triangular-sectioned head (many of the barbs are now damaged). Arrowheads of this form are relatively well represented on Roman military sites, both continental and British. In Scotland they have been found at Newstead and Bar Hill, in both cases in the well in the headquarters building, while at Bar Hill fragments of horn from the composite bows of horn and sinew which were used with them were also recovered. The archers of the Roman army were predominantly recruited in the eastern provinces, especially Syria. Although the auxiliary unit which used these arrowheads at Newstead is unknown, a cohort of archers from the Syrian town of Hama is attested at Bar Hill.

FRA 211, 214, 216.
Curle 1911, 189, pl XXXVIII; Robertson, Scott & Keppie 1975, 56, 58, fig 18. 99, 101, fig 32; Davies 1977

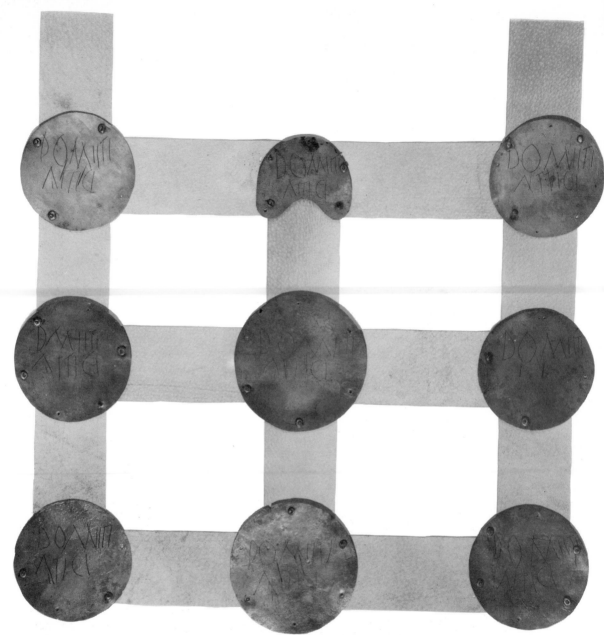

8 Bronze back-plates for *phalerae*

Late 1st century AD
Newstead, Roxburghshire—a Roman fort
D (of largest disc)   115mm

These plates, eight of which are circular and one is kidney-shaped, are best interpreted as the backing for metal *phalerae*. The *phalerae* themselves, which were badges of military distinction, were often highly decorated. They were worn on the breast on a leather harness. On the basis of these pieces it would seem that the *phalerae* were held in place on the leather by being rivetted to back-plates. All of the nine plates have remains of such rivets or the holes for them but in different numbers—the larger of the circular examples had six rivets while the smaller had four and the kidney-shaped piece had five. All of the pieces have the name of their owner, DOMITIVS ATTICVS, scratched on them.

FRA 129
Curle 1911, 174–77, pl XXXI

The iron flask is shown with a 19th century example made largely of wood. The latter has the following inscription: Private T Clarke, 54th Regiment, Sebastopol, Crimea.

9 Iron flask

2nd century AD
Newstead, Roxburghshire—a Roman fort
D   45mm

The body of the circular flask has been made in two identical halves, joined together by a slight overlap. On the top a separate bronze collar and a pair of broad bronze straps terminating in decorative bronze plates have been soldered onto the iron. Slots in these plates would have held some fitting to take a handle or leather strap. The neck is now broken but would have been rather longer and fitted with a stopper or cap. Examples of metal flasks are extremely rare and there are no close parallels for this particular find.

FRA 3435
Close-Brooks forthcoming

10   Pickaxe (*dolabra*)

Late 1st–2nd century AD
Newstead, Roxburghshire—a Roman fort
L   435mm

The curved pick, which is chisel-edged and hexagonal in cross-section, is balanced by the axe blade and there are lugs on either side of the eye for the handle. Damage to the edges of both the axe and the pick testify to considerable use. The handle, which is here restored, was probably ash to judge from the single example from Newstead where part of the handle was preserved. This pickaxe is one of five which were found in Pit XVI; on the upper edge of another is stamped, ATTICVS, presumably the name of the toolmaker. The scenes on Trajan's Column suggest that these pickaxes were used for a wide variety of heavy work and may even on occasion have been used as weapons.

FRA 227
Curle 1911, 278–79, pl LVII; Manning 1976, 27–28

III PARADE EQUIPMENT

Some of the more elaborate pieces could never have been
used in battle. They were designed for elaborate parades and
mock-battles which were an important element in the
ceremonial side of army life.

Photograph by Courtesy of The Scotsman.

11 Brass helmet

Late 1st century AD
Newstead, Roxburghshire—a Roman fort
H   255mm   *Plate 1*

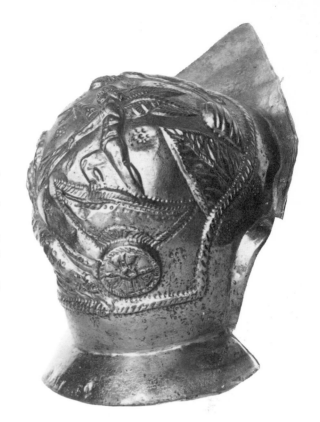

The top and the back of the helmet are covered with embossed decoration. On the back is a cupid in a 2-wheeled chariot driving a pair of leopards. Behind the cupid there is a large palm-leaf and two ribbed, cone-like objects which cannot now be identified. On the crown another cupid flies along with arms outstretched and with his legs and feet towards the peak. The peak and the neck-guard are plain but the latter carries an inscription of eight punched letters—only the last four, TGES, are now legible. There are traces of a leather lining on the inside of the helmet. Although there are no rivet-holes for its attachment it seems likely that the helmet would have had a face-mask, perhaps fixed to the two small projections on either side of the peak.

FRA 125
Curle 1911, 166–68, pl XXVI–XXVIII; Toynbee 1962, 166, pl 106; Robinson 1975, 112–13, pl 314–16; Garbsch 1978, 57, taf 12.2

12 Bronze helmet-mask

Late 1st century AD
Newstead, Roxburghshire—a Roman fort
H   210mm

Beaten out of bronze, this face-mask is all that remains of the helmet. The beardless face is young and rather idealised but the most notable feature is the thick roll of hair above the brow. The elaborately waved hair is divided into four segments by three vertical plaits. At each end of this roll four wavy locks hang down either cheek, in front of the imitation-ears, below each of which is a rivet-hole for the attachment of the helmet.

FRA 123
Curle 1911, 170–71, pl XXX; Toynbee 1962, 167, pl 105; Robinson 1975, 124, pl 359–60; Garbsch 1978, 57, taf 24.1

13   Iron helmet

Late 1st century AD
Newstead, Roxburghshire—a Roman fort
H   245mm

This example, which retains traces of silver-plating, has both the mask and the helmet surviving although the line where the two parts joined is now missing as is the right side of the face. The face is youthful and effeminate with a cluster of spiral curls hanging down each cheek in front of the ear. The crown and back of the head are covered with tight, spiral curls, radiating from a central 'star-fish' and confined by a laurel-wreath. On the neck-guard is a pattern of dots and zig-zags. Underneath it is an inscription in punched letters, and the number XXII incised. There are attachments for streamers and two tubular plume-holders. Traces of woollen lining or padding still remain on the inner surfaces.

FRA 124
Curle 1911, 168–69, pl XXVI, XXIX; Toynbee 1962, 167, pl 104; Robinson 1975, 115–16, pl 318–19; Garbsch 1978, 57

A reconstruction of the chamfron

14 Leather chamfron

Late 1st century AD
Newstead, Roxburghshire—a Roman fort
H   570mm

Although found in several pieces, sufficient survives of this horse's headpiece to enable it to be reconstructed. It is made from two pieces of leather—an upper thick layer and a backing of finer and thinner material. The whole of the surface is covered with a design executed partly by tooling and partly by inserting brass-headed studs of three different sizes. The motifs used include circles, semi-circles and leaves. The eyeholes would have been filled with pierced globular bronze eye-guards

FRA 74
Curle 1911, 153–55, pl XXI; 1913, 400–05; Robinson 1975, 190, pl 514, 516

25

IV TENTS

These were only used when the army was campaigning or on summer exercises away from the permanent forts.

Army Camp at Selkirk, about 1915.

15 Fragments of leather tents

Late 1st–2nd century AD
Newstead, Roxburghshire—a Roman fort
W (of largest fragment) 70mm

Although not recognised as such at the time, the excavations at Newstead produced a large number of fragments from leather tents. They were constructed from a large number of pieces of leather, usually calf, sewn together. The tent for the ordinary soldier had the form of a modern ridge-tent, although the officers tents would have been more elaborate. As well as the larger fragments, the positions of which are shown on the diagram, the finds also included circular or pear-shaped pieces which were applied to the main body of the tent and acted as attachment points for the guy-ropes.

FRA 13, 21, 44, 62, 73
Curle 1911, 149–50, pl XIX; McIntyre & Richmond 1934; Groenman-van Waateringe 1967

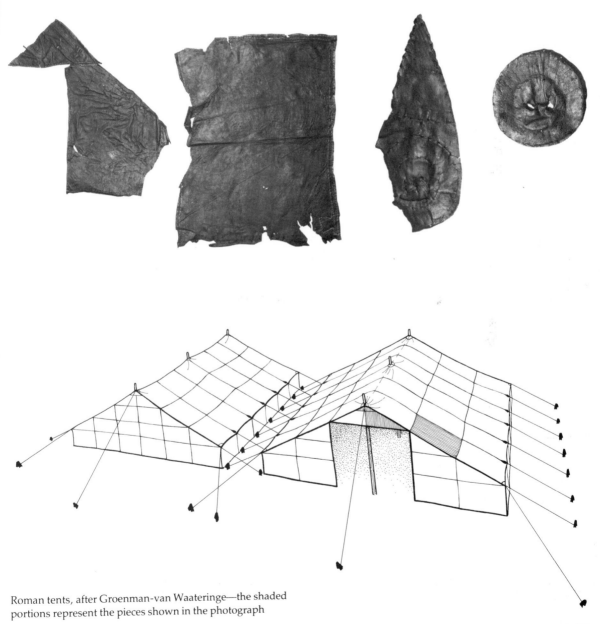

Roman tents, after Groenman-van Waateringe—the shaded portions represent the pieces shown in the photograph

16 Mallet-head

Late 1st century AD
Newstead, Roxburghshire—a Roman fort
L 192mm

Found in pit LIV this wooden mallet-head is a rare example of what, at the time, must have been a common tool. The handle is restored.

FRA 1141
Curle 1911, 280, pl LXXXIII

17 Tent-pegs

Late 1st century AD
Newstead, Roxburghshire—a Roman fort
L (of the largest example) 480mm

Numerous examples were recovered from the ditch of the early fort. They are made of oak and are triangular in section with points at both ends and a well-defined notch for the attachment of the ropes. Recent experiments suggest they would have been made of seasoned timber, split with a bill-hook and maul and finally trimmed into shape with a bill-hook. It would not have taken more than 2 or 3 minutes to make a single peg. The sharp points at both ends indicate that the Newstead examples were unused. Comparable tent-pegs are known from Coelbren, Glamorgan and Melandra Castle, Glossop, Derbyshire.

FRA 1151
Curle 1911, 310 & pl LXXXIII; Wild 1974

V BUILDINGS

18 Iron nails

Late 1st century AD
Inchtuthil, Perthshire—a Roman
legionary fortress
L (of longest example)   300mm

A hoard of over 875,000 nails was found during the excavations. They were buried in a pit 3.6m deep specially dug for the purpose and were covered by 1.8m of clean beaten earth. The nails vary in length from 380mm to 63mm, the smaller ones being much the more common. The buildings of the fortress, which were still being constructed at the time of its abandonment, were all timber-framed and these nails represented the stockpile for future work. Clearly, the quantity involved was too great for removal at the time of abandonment and they were therefore buried to prevent the iron falling into the hands of the native population.

FY 169–82
Angus, Brown & Cleere 1962

19 Stamped tile (*imbrex*)

Early 3rd century AD
Carpow, Perthshire—a Roman fortress
L 216mm

Parts of over 200 stamped tiles were found during the excavations in 1961–62 but on only two fragments, of which this is one, was the inscription preserved complete. It reads LEG·VI·VIC·B·P·F and shows them to have been made by the Legion VI Victrix, which was normally based at York. The additional title PF, standing for *pia fidelis*, was aquired by the legion in the 1st century AD for its loyalty to Domitian while B, an abbreviation for *Britannica*, represents a fresh honour conferred on the legion for its efforts in the campaigns, led by the Emperor Severus, which preceded the building of the fortress at Carpow. All the stamps on the tiles come from one or other of two dies and they may well have been made locally.

FRC 1
Birley 1963, 200, pl XXIII. 3; Wright 1976, 233, 229, fig 4.62

20 Window glass

Mid 2nd century AD
Rough Castle, Stirlingshire—a Roman fort on the Antonine Wall
H (of fragment) 185mm

Fragments of window glass are common enough finds on the sites of Roman forts but nowhere in Scotland has it been possible to estimate the size of the pane. Nor is it clear exactly how the panes were secured in the window-frames but it seems likely that cement was used in place of putty. Two alternative methods of manufacture have been suggested and both may have been in use— one involves casting the panes in moulds while the other requires the blown glass to be formed into a cylinder which is subsequently cut and flattened.

FR 377
Buchanan, Christison & Anderson 1905, 493; Haevernick & Hahn-Weinheimer 1955; Harden 1961; Boon 1966

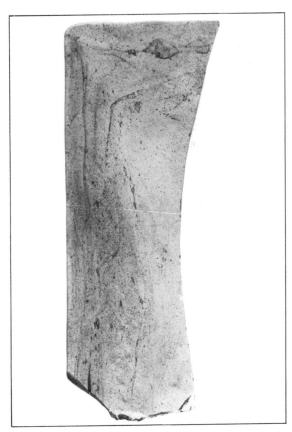

VI FURNITURE

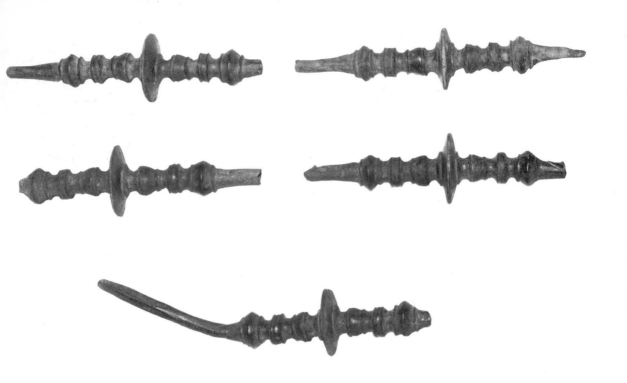

21 Folding stool

Late 1st century AD
Newstead, Roxburghshire—a Roman fort
L (of the longest rod)   260mm

Among the numerous pits found at Newstead,
one contained what appeared to be the stock in
trade of a smith and included the five iron rods
shown here. Although they are now of varying
lengths it can be readily appreciated that they
form a set. They are decorated with a series of
hammered mouldings while at the central point
there is a large disc and they are clearly intended
to simulate turned woodwork. A further plain
bar of iron, of which one survives, was to be
attached to either end. On the basis of the more
complete find from Nijmegen in Holland, there
can be little doubt that these form part of the
framework of a folding stool with curved
wooden legs and a leather or canvas seat. The
length of the stool is likely to have been about
460mm.

FRA 311
*Curle 1911, 268–87, LXIV; Liversidge 1955, 33–34,
pl 39*

A reconstruction of the folding stool from Nijmegen

C

22 Stone bench support

2nd century AD
Mumrills, Stirlingshire—a Roman fort on
the Antonine Wall
H 400mm

The piece is plain apart from the front edge
which has been hollowed to a depth of 100mm.
At the top and bottom of this hollow are simple
mouldings. It was found in the changing room,
one of the rooms in the bath-house—the very
considerable heat and moisture in these rooms
would have made stone furniture essential. The
seat is a modern reconstruction.

FRB 607
Macdonald & Curle 1929, 453 & 414, fig 11b

VII TEXTILES AND CLOTHING

This is poorly represented but only exceptional burial
conditions will preserve traces of organic material such as
wool or leather.

23 Wooden spindle

Late 1st century AD
Newstead, Roxburghshire—a Roman fort
L   155mm

It is a narrow rod of wood with a symmetrical thickening near the lower end to hold the spindle-whorl. The wood of this example has not been identified but box-wood was the favoured material in Roman times. The whorl which is a disc-shaped weight, pierced with a central hole so that it can be impaled on the lower end of the spindle and rammed tight on the thickened bulb, adds momentum to the rotation of the spindle and is essential to successful spinning. The process of spinning using a spindle and whorl has been described in detail by Catullus and is still to be observed in many parts of the world. The prepared fibres, usually combed wool, are first attached to a long rod or distaff. The distaff is held in the left hand and taking a few fibres from the bottom of the mass between the wetted forefinger and thumb of the right hand the spinner simultaneously twists them together and draws them gently downwards. Once the thread is long enough it is tied to the top of the spindle, which is then vigorously rotated. The thread then hangs perpendicularly from the mass of fibres on the distaff with the free rotating spindle at the end of it. With the fingers of the right hand the spinner continues to draw out a controlled number of fibres from the distaff and these are twisted by the action of the spindle into a thread. The thread is stretched and made finer by the weight of the spindle. The process continues until the spindle reaches the floor and stops and at this point the spinner picks up the spindle and, using it as a bobbin, winds up the spun thread. The thread is then fastened to the top of the spindle and the process begins again. When the spindle is full of yarn, the thread is broken off and wound into a ball or onto a bobbin.

FRA 461
Curle 1911, 290, pl LXVIII; Wild 1970, 32–33, 35–37, 127

24 Fragments of cloth

2nd century AD
Newstead, Roxburghshire—a Roman fort
L (of largest fragment)   130mm

These two small fragments of woollen cloth in plain weave are the only known examples from a Roman fort in Scotland.

FRA 1180
Curle 1911, 289; Henshall 1952, 8; Wild 1970, 91

25 Fragment of cloth

Mid 3rd century AD
Falkirk, Stirlingshire
L   110mm

This small fragment of herringbone or weft-chevron twill has a simple check design. The checks are achieved by using yarns of two colours, light yellow brown and dark chocolate brown. Both colours are found as natural pigments in the wool of the Soay sheep and undyed yarns in natural colours had the advantage of being fast to washing. Such checks were popular amongst the native population in the northern Roman provinces and seem to have been invented by them in the pre-Roman period. This fragment was found stopping the mouth of a jar containing a large coin hoard (see no 48).

FR 483
Wild 1970, 23, 48, 53, 96–97, figs 23, 48, pl VIb

26 Leather shoes

Late 1st–2nd century AD
Newstead, Roxburghshire—a Roman fort
L (of largest shoe)   250mm

A number of shoes, some largely complete and some fragmentary, were found during the excavations at Newstead. A variety of styles is represented varying from the simple examples made from a single piece of leather to those with heavy, studded soles and elaborately cut-out uppers. Those belonging to the soldiers cannot be distinguished from those of civilians. Equally, it is not generally possible to tell whether the shoes were for men or women. Some, from their size, must have been for children.

FRA 77, 78, 96, 108, 114
Curle 1911, 150–53, pl XX

VIII JEWELLERY

27 Brooch

Late 2nd–early 3rd century AD (date of
manufacture).
Carlungie, Angus—a native settlement
W 51mm

This bronze brooch is decorated with glass and
enamel set in prepared hollows. Cast in one
piece it has 4 circles in the form of a cross with
narrow leaf-shaped panels between each circle.
Two small knobs were originally attached to the
outside of each circle and these, together with
the leaf panels, held blue glass inlays secured by
a flux of red enamel. After they were inserted
these inlays have been ground flush with the
edges of the bronze hollows. The circles contain
enamel, probably pale-yellow originally, in
which is set 13-15 opaque white glass circlets. On
the back of the brooch there are the remains of a
broken pin. The piece is Gallo-Roman, probably
made in Northern France or Belgium. It was
found during the excavation of an underground
chamber (souterrain) at Carlungie.

HD 1739
Wainwright 1953, 68–70, pl 16a

28 Penannular Brooch

2nd century AD
Newstead, Roxburghshire—a Roman fort
W (of penannular ring)   50mm

The brooch has a largely plain penannular
bronze ring with blunt, expanded terminals.
These terminals are decorated with a dog-tooth
ornament and a broken-backed curve and both
decorative elements are emphasised by silver
inlay. The pin, which is free to rotate around
most of the ring, is also made of bronze and
slightly curved with a markedly flat and
expanded tip. This type of brooch has a much
earlier origin and several Scottish examples are
datable to the preceding Iron Age. As well as
being one of the most elaborate, this brooch is
also one of the latest of its type in date and seems
to have been made when the style was going out
of fashion—other forms of penannular brooch
continued well into the post-Roman period.

FRA 806
*Curle 1911, 327, pl LXXXVIII; MacGregor 1976,
126 & 120, fig 5. 9*

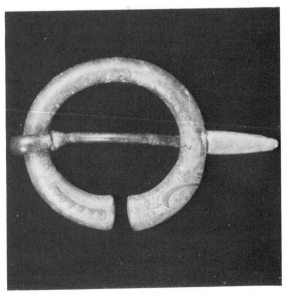

29 Intaglio ring

Early 1st century AD
Arthur's Seat, Edinburgh—a native settlement
L (of stone)   19mm

The ring is typical of the Augustan period and resembles several found in the Rhineland so that by the time of the Agricolan advance into Scotland it may have been almost a century old. The stone has the profile bust of an ephebe, wearing an Athenian helmet with raised visor and long horse hair plume. This can be identified as a representation of Alexander the Great— idealised heroic heads were often worn as amulets. The engraving is skilfully done and, although there are provincial shortcomings, a Mediterranean origin seems likely. Two iron stumps are all that remain of the ring.

FT 97
Henig 1970; Stevenson 1970

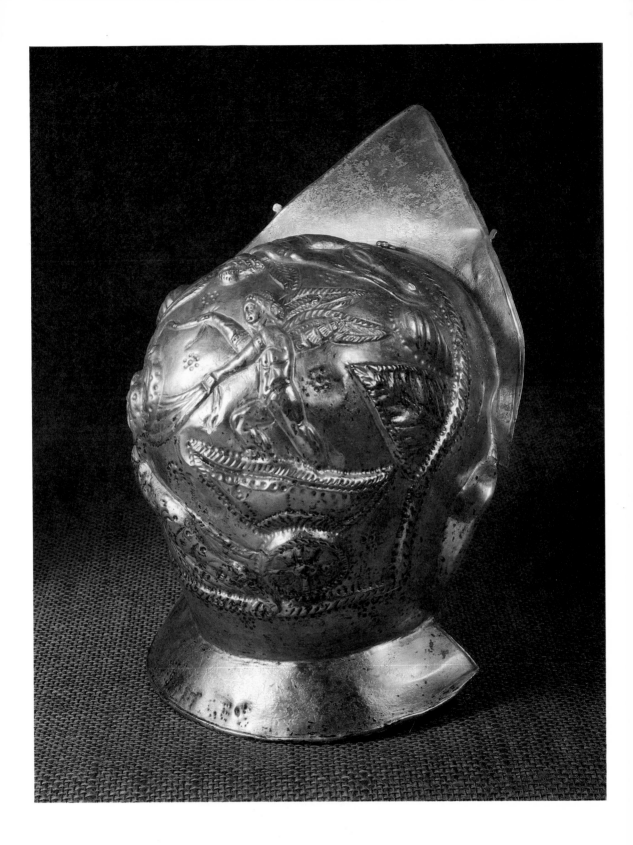

Plate 1

Plate 2

Plate 3

Plate 4

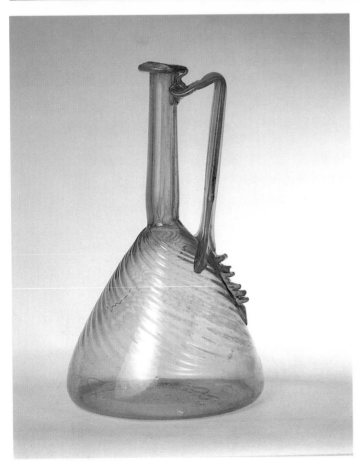

Plate 5

Plate 6

30 Silver necklace

Late 1st–2nd century AD
Newstead, Roxburghshire—a Roman fort
W (of wheel)   27mm

The necklace consists of a silver chain joined to either side of a miniature nine-spoked wheel in silver filigree. There is a terminal hook for the chain from which a small crescent-shaped pendant hung. The chain, which was about 250mm in length, is now very brittle and much decayed. Although found near the same spot, the wheel was not discovered at the same time as the chain and therefore cannot be certainly associated with it—there seems, however, every reason to believe that they all form part of a single piece. The wheel and crescent, symbols for the sun and moon respectively, were worn as amulets to promote good luck and ward off evil spirits. Although pre-Roman in origin the wheel as a symbol for the sun became, in Roman times, linked with Jupiter. Several examples of model wheels have been found in the civilian areas of southern Britain.

FRA 851
Curle 1911, 333–35, pl LXXXVII; Green 1976

31 Bone pin

Late 1st century AD
Newstead, Roxburghshire—a Roman fort
L   114mm

The head of this perfectly preserved pin is a carefully executed bust intended to represent a lady, perhaps an Empress or Princess of the period, with a high and elaborate hair-style.

FRA 688
Curle 1911, 337 & pl XCIII; Toynbee 1964, 360

IX COOKING AND TABLEWARE

Rather surprisingly Roman forts had no large mess halls.
Cooking was the responsibility of the soldiers who probably
organised it on the basis of members of a single barrack-
block or barrack room.

32 Mess cans

Late 1st–2nd century AD
Newstead, Roxburghshire—a Roman fort
H (of largest example)   240mm   *Plate 2*

These bronze vessels were probably an
important part of the ordinary soldier's cooking
equipment. All show considerable signs of wear
and most have been mended by means of
rivetted patches. Only traces of the iron handles
now survive. Several of the vessels bear
scratched or punched inscriptions identifying
either the owner or his unit.

FRA 1185–91
*Curle 1911, 273–74, pl LIII; Eggers 1966, 109,
123–24, abb 16–17*

33 Grid-iron

Late 1st century AD
Newstead, Roxburghshire—a Roman fort
W   305mm   *Plate 2*

The sides and legs are each made from a single
strip of iron and there are eight bars forming the
grid.

FRA 1184
Curle 1911, 274, pl LIII

34 Samian ware

Late 1st–2nd century AD
Newstead, Roxburghshire—a Roman fort
W (of largest bowl)   240mm   *Plate 3*

Samian ware is a distinctive type of fine, red
pottery made to imitate metal vessels. It was
made in large quantities at various sites in France
and exported all over the Empire. Because of the
industrial nature of the production the forms,
though varied, are extremely standardised. Both
plain and decorated forms are found and both
are often stamped with the name of the maker —
the large hemispherical bowl, for example, has
the name CINNAMVS running vertically down it
as part of the decoration (the bowl containing
pears in the photograph). The decorated pots
were made in clay moulds in which each motif
was separately stamped. This technique, in
which each motif had a separate stamp, meant
that a bewildering variety of combinations of
motifs was possible. The standardised forms, the
names of the makers and the occurrence of
individual motifs on several different pots enable
samian ware to be more closely dated than other
forms of Roman pottery.

FRA 1249, 1322, 1339, 1350, 1352, 1354, 1356, 1362
Curle 1911, 190–242; Hartley 1969

35 Coarse pottery

Late 1st–2nd century AD
Newstead, Roxburghshire, except for b,
Camelon, Stirlingshire—Roman forts
Plate 4

Coarse pottery is the term used to include all
forms of pottery other than samian ware and
some of it is of very high quality. The Roman
forts in Scotland were supplied from kilns
situated all over Britain.

a. Cup decorated with hunting scenes
   H   120mm   FRA 1391
b. Cup with rough-cast decorative surface
   H   125mm   FX 23

c. Dish with straight, upright sides in a burnished black fabric
D 280mm   FRA 1406

d. Wide-mouthed bowl with a single groove encircling the widest part of the body
H 100mm   FRA 1400

e. Bowl imitating the samian ware form Dragendorff 30
H 95mm   FRA 1396

f. *Mortarium* or mixing bowl, the inner surface studded with grits. On the rim is the stamp of the maker, BRVSC(IVS).
D 295mm   FRA 1428

g. Flagon in a cream ware
H 290mm   FRA 1421

h. Narrow-mouthed jar with two handles and two settings for securing a lid
H 235mm   FRA 1365

i. Jar with rusticated surface
H 175mm   FRA 1369

j. Jar with simple, burnished lattice decoration on the upper part of the body
H 280mm   FRA 1364

Curle 1911, 243–70; Gillam 1957

36   Glass jug

2nd century AD
Brackenbraes, Turriff, Aberdeenshire
H 224mm   *Plate 5*

This jug, which is made of blown green glass, has a long narrow neck with a marked constriction at its base and a conical body. The rim is folded outward and flattened horizontally. The body is decorated with fine diagonal ribbing while on the handle there is a more pronounced vertical rib. Complete glass vessels of this date are rare except from burials but there is no evidence that this particular example accompanied one. It was found in a sandy hillock which had been partly cut away during the construction of the Inveramsay to Turriff railway between 1855 and 1857. A large number of glass beads were found with it but none of these now survive.

FR 484
Dunbar 1930; Curle 1932, 291, 389; Isings 1957, 72–73

37   Bronze skillet (*patera*)

Late 1st–early 2nd century AD
West Lothian
L 197mm

The skillet was made initially in three pieces, the handle and the base having been separately fashioned before being joined to the bowl. The decoration is in green, red and blue champleve enamel, in part forming a background to reserved designs. Running round the exterior of the bowl are three main decorative zones—a wreath, a vine-scroll and a ray pattern. The upper surface of the flat handle has vine leaves and scroll ornaments, although the enamel is here a restoration. The form of the skillet is Roman as are the decorative motifs which derive from samian ware bowls but the enamel technique is Celtic—although these skillets are conveniently referred to as being enamelled this is technically incorrect since they do not have true enamels but only coloured glass which has not fused with the bronzework. Only a small number of these vessels are known, of which this is one of the finest examples, and they are widely scattered over much of Europe. The closest parallels to this particular skillet have been found at Braughing in Hertfordshire, Maltboek in Jutland and Nehasitz in Bohemia. It seems likely that they were the product of British workshops with some being exported to the Continent.

FR 43
Toynbee 1962, 174 & pl 125; Moore 1978

38   Bronze skillet (*patera*)

1st century AD
Dowalton Loch crannog, Wigtownshire
—a native settlement
L 393mm

This otherwise plain skillet has a decorative ring-handle attached below the rim of the bowl opposite the flat handle. The movable ring represents a very stylised wreath ending in two equally stylised heads of monsters. This wreath frames a Medusa mask applied to the surface of the bowl. The interior is tinned and is engraved

with a series of circles, presumably for
measuring purposes. The handle bears the
stamp of the Italian bronze-founder, Publius
Cipius Polibius.

HU 1
*Toynbee 1964, 321 & pl 75c (detail of ring handle
only); Curle 1932, 299–300, figs 10–11*

39 Bronze jug

Late 1st century AD
Newstead, Roxburghshire—a Roman fort
H   280mm

This capacious jug is plain apart from the elaborately decorated handle. At the junction with the rim there is a projecting lotus-bud between two birds' heads that run along the edge to the left and right. At the base of the handle there is a head of Bacchus with ivy tendrils wreathed in his hair. Both this jug and the following example (no 40) are likely to be imports from Italy.

FRA 1193
Curle 1911, 275, pl LV; Toynbee 1964, 323

40 Bronze jug

Late 1st century AD
Newstead, Roxburghshire—a Roman for
H   300mm

Around the body is a band of well-executed lotu pattern while on the turned-over rim is a border of small ovolos. Where the handle joins the rim there are two heads of long-beaked water-birds emerging from a bunch of pointed leaves or a flower while the other end of the handle has a female head with the hair braided and hanging in long curls on either side. There are traces of silver inlay, particularly in the eyes of the female head at the base of the handle and in the lotus pattern round the body.

FRA 1194
Curle 1911, 275–76, fig 38, pl LVI; Toynbee 1964, 323

X MEDICINE

Keeping the soldiers healthy was an important element in all
Roman army procedures. In addition there was a good
medical service and at several Scottish forts, including
Fendoch and Inchtuthil, hospitals have been found.

Chemist's shop at Aberfeldy, Perthshire, 1973.

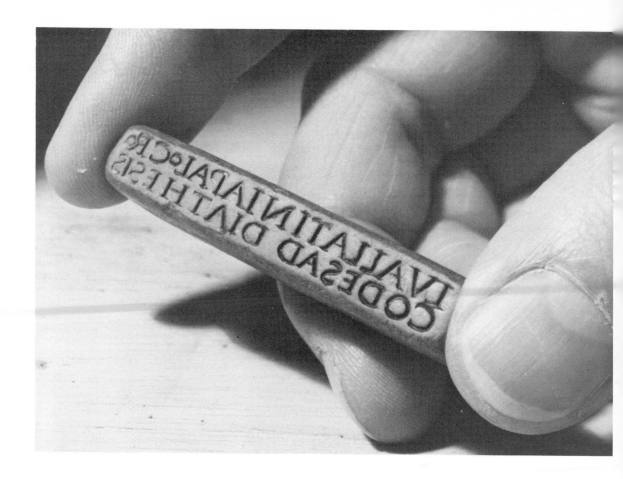

41 Oculist's stamp

2nd century AD
Tranent, East Lothian
L 60mm

The stamp is made of greenish steatite in the form of a parallelogram. On one edge it carries the inscription L VALLATINI APALOCROCODES AD DIATHESIS while on the opposite it is L VALLATINI EVODES AD CICATRICES ET ASP(E)RITVDIN(ES). These inscriptions may be translated as Lucius Vallatinus' mild *crocodes* for infections of the eyes and *evodes* for cicatrices and granulations. *Evodes* probably stands for collyrium, a form of eye-wash lotion, while *crocodes* contains saffron as one of its principal ingredients. The stamp would have been used by the oculist to mark the wax or other material sealing the packages he had prepared.

FT 25
Curle 1932, 354

42 Folding bronze spoon

2nd–3rd century AD
Traprain Law, East Lothian—a native hillfort
L 106mm

The handle represents an outstretched lion between whose paws an L-shaped projection from the bowl of the spoon has been hinged so that it folds back and upwards over the lion's head. The other end of the handle is fan-shaped, split on one side and provided with a small hole. This may perhaps have been to take a lancet or needle lying along the right-hand side of the handle resting on a catch near the lion's head. The underside of the handle is hollow to hold perhaps a probe or scoop, and a hinge is provided below the fan-shaped terminal. The bowl is of the so-called fiddle-shaped form. Only ten of these spoons have been recorded from Britian and on none of them have the implements that fitted onto the handles

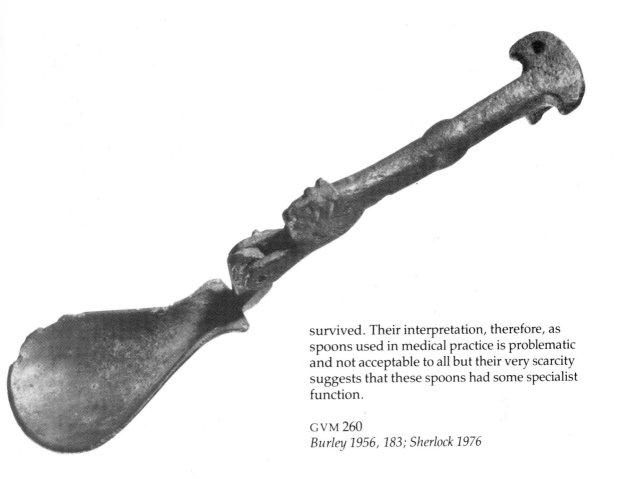

survived. Their interpretation, therefore, as spoons used in medical practice is problematic and not acceptable to all but their very scarcity suggests that these spoons had some specialist function.

GVM 260
Burley 1956, 183; Sherlock 1976

43 Inscribed amphora sherd

Early 3rd century AD
Carpow, Perthshire—a Roman fortress
H   75mm

The fragment appears to come from a cylindrical wine-amphora but its interest derives from a graffito in Greek capitals incised after firing. Sufficient survives, ΠΡΑΣΙ . . ., as to leave no doubt that the amphora originally contained wine flavoured with horehound, a cough medicine. Dioscurides, writing in the 1st century AD, gives a prescription for wine flavoured with horehound for use in the treatment of chest complaints and the remedy was still used in this century. Found during the excavations at the fortress; the fact that the graffito is in Greek implies that the medical officer based there could speak Greek or was perhaps of Greek origin.

FRC 33
Birley 1963, 202; Davies 1970, 92 & 94, fig 10

XI WRITING

The Romans introduced writing into Scotland.

The Letter-writer. Cartoon by Rowlandson, 1815.

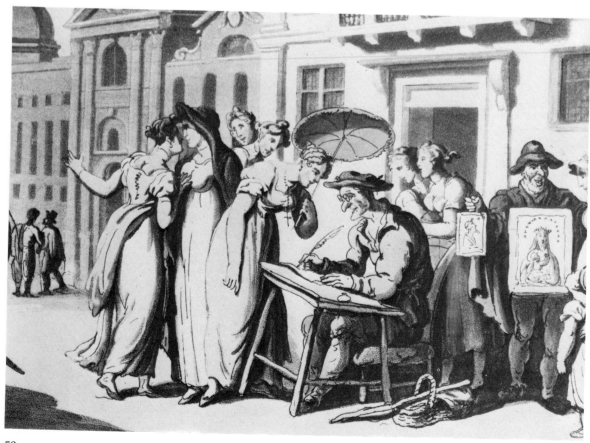

44 Writing tablet

Mid 2nd century AD
Newstead, Roxburghshire—a Roman fort
L   135mm

This writing tablet, probably one of a pair, is made of pine. A single sheet of wood has been used with the central area hollowed out for the insertion of a wax tablet on which the message was written. When ready for despatch a pair of writing tablets could be closed up like a book, tied up with string and secured by a seal-box.

FRA 710
Curle 1911, 308

45 Iron *stylus*

Late 1st century AD
Newstead, Roxburghshire—a Roman fort
L   138mm

The *stylus* was the normal writing implement used in Roman times. With the sharp point messages could be scratched in the wax of the writing tablet (see no 44) while the broad end acted as an eraser. Iron *styli* are rarer and simpler in form than bronze examples. They had to be forged individually so that ornamentation was much more difficult and time-consuming whereas decorative bronze *styli* were easily cast. Some of the iron *styli* from Newstead appear to have been designed to have a separately fitted point, perhaps of agate.

FRA 706
Curle 1911, 307–08, pl LXXX; Manning 1976, 34

The complete writing tablet is a reconstruction based on the example from Newstead

46 Amphora sherd

Late 1st–2nd century AD
Newstead, Roxburghshire—a Roman fort
H (of the sherd)   150mm

Writing on most amphorae takes the form of a
stamped or scratched inscription. This is a much
more unusual example where the letters have
been painted on instead. What survives reads

APRILIS

HEL . . .

and probably represents the name of the trader
whose products were contained in the amphora.

FRA 1434
Curle 1911, pl LII

47 Inscribed stone

2nd–4th century AD
Traprain Law, East Lothian—a native
hillfort
L   34mm

The stone has a rounded end and on the surface
are incised the letters A B C and a portion of D. It
is not unreasonable to suppose that when
complete the stone contained the whole
alphabet. Certainly, it implies some interest on
the part of the native population in the Romans'
ability to write.

GV 1922.273
Cree & Curle 1922, 256, 231, fig 27.1

XII MONEY

The Romans brought the first coins in any quantity to
Scotland.

48 Coin hoard

Mid 3rd century AD (date of burial)
Falkirk, Stirlingshire
H (of pot) 210mm *Plate 6*

The hoard of almost 2,000 silver *denarii* contained in a pot was found during the levelling of ground. The mouth of the pot had been stopped with cloth (see no 25). More than 300 years had elapsed between the minting of the oldest coin and the most recent in the hoard—the earliest was struck around 83 BC and the latest in 230 AD.

Virtually every emperor between Nero (54-68 AD) and Alexander Severus (222-235 AD) is represented among the coins. This considerable range suggests that the hoard had been accumulated over several generations, probably by a family of wealthy merchants in the native population. The latest coins, which were minted after the Romans left Scotland, show that contacts were maintained with the area to the south still under Roman control.

FR 482
Macdonald 1934b; 1934c

Some of the coins from the hoard—*top left*, Nero (54–68 AD); *top right*, Antoninus Pius (138–161 AD); *bottom left*, Crispina, wife of Commodus (177–192 AD); *bottom right*, Alexander Severus (222–235 AD).

XIII AGRICULTURE

49 Iron spade sheath

2nd century AD
Rough Castle, Stirlingshire—a Roman
fort on the Antonine Wall
L   175mm

This iron spade sheath falls into the round
mouthed category—that is, the groove which
provides a seating for the wooden spade is
strongly curved and the sheath itself terminates
in outward flaring arms. It can be compared with
a similar example from Malton, Yorkshire.

FR 385
*Buchanan, Christison & Anderson 1905, 495;
Manning 1970, 22, fig 2.m; Corder 1948, 177, fig 3*

A wooden spade with an iron edge

50 Rake

Late 1st century AD
Newstead, Roxburghshire—a Roman fort
L   325mm

The piece comprises an oak clog through which
seven slightly curved iron prongs project. These
are held fast at the opposite end where they are
doubled over the lower edge of the clog. Such
composite rakes seem to be usual in Roman
Britain, although examples with wooden prongs
may also have existed. The handle is restored.

FRA 292
Curle 1911, 283, pl LXI; Manning 1966, 10

51 Antler rake

Mid 2nd century AD
Newstead, Roxburghshire—a Roman fort
L   300mm

This implement, from pit XCVIII, is formed from
the burr of a red deer antler with the brow and
bez tines. A hole has been made just above the
burr, through the base of the beam. The wooden
handle is restored.

FRA 1160
Curle 1913, 287, fig 7; Bagshawe 1949

52 Iron turf cutter

Late 1st–2nd century AD
Newstead, Roxburghshire—a Roman fort
L   150mm

This anchor-shaped knife was probably
employed to cut turfs used in the construction of
ramparts, and possibly also for cutting peats for
fuel. However, unlike true peat spades, moon-
shaped turf cutters could only be used in
conjunction with spades. The handle is a
restoration. Similar pieces have been found at
Silchester, Woodyates, and Housesteads.

FRA 291
*Curle 1911, 284, pl LXI; Manning 1966, 26; 1976,
28, fig 18.80; Pitt-Rivers 1892, 139, pl CLXXXIV.9*

53 Iron scythe blade

Late 1st century AD
Newstead, Roxburghshire—a Roman fort
L 975mm

An anchor-shaped rivet probably served to fasten the blade to its single long handle. The blade itself, although large, is relatively short and broad. The handle is an experimental restoration, curved to put the blade at a correct cutting angle. This type of scythe was undoubtedly first introduced to Britain by the Romans. The Carlingwark Loch hoard, Kirkcudbrightshire produced fragments which are probably of this type. The Roman forts at Bar Hill and Loudoun Hill yielded more certain examples.

FRA 288
Curle 1911, 284, pl LXII. 4; Macdonald 1934a, 515; Manning 1976

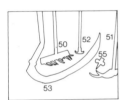

54 Iron tanged reaping hook

Late 1st century AD
Newstead, Roxburghshire—a Roman fort
L 150mm

The edge of the blade lies to one side of the handle and therefore cannot be swung like a sickle. This one is a later type with a strong concave curve to the narrow blade. It appears that the edges have been strengthened with steel. The handle is a modern restoration. A hook of exactly this pattern is illustrated on Trajan's Column, held in the right hand of a legionary about to cut the ears of corn in his left hand. The hook is comparable with examples from Carlingwark Loch, Kirkcudbrightshire, Wilsford Down, Wiltshire, and Risingham, Northumberland.

FRA 282
Curle 1911, 284, pl LXI; Cunnington & Goddard 1934, 231, pl LXXVII.9; Manning 1976, 30, fig 19.83; Piggott 1953, 35, fig 9

55 Mower's anvil

Late 1st century AD
Newstead, Roxburghshire—a Roman fort
L 150mm

The mower's anvil is a solid iron peg, pointed at the end to be driven into the ground. A strip of iron, bent into a spiral, passes through a hole 65mm from the top of the peg and prevents the anvil from sinking any deeper into the ground. A mower would lay his scythe blade across the 45mm square end to hammer its edges before finally polishing it with a hone. A similar example was found at Silchester. Mower's anvils are no longer used in Britain but are in use in many parts of Europe and South America.

FRA 287
Curle 1911, 284, pl LXII; Boon 1957, 182, fig 35.13

56 Bucket

Late 1st century AD
Newstead, Roxburghshire—a Roman fort
H 310mm

The staves of the bucket are made of oak while the base appears to be of pine. It is held together with two iron hoops, one of which is modern. Two iron plates run up the sides of the bucket to support the handle.

FRA 1201
Curle 1911, 310, pl LXIX

XIV CRAFTS

The Roman army units, especially the legions, included
numerous craftsmen who combined their skills with
soldiering.

THE BLACKSMITH

57 Fire shovel

2nd century AD
Newstead, Roxburghshire—a Roman fort
L   700mm

This fire shovel was fashioned by the blacksmith with a twisted handle and a hammered out terminal to ensure a firmer grip. It was used by the blacksmith in the furnace. Others come from Verulamium (modern St Albans) and the Carrawburgh Mithraeum.

FRA 321
Curle 1913, 388, fig 2; Frere 1972, 164, fig 60.6; Manning 1976, 39, fig 23. 149

58 Smith's rake

Late 1st–2nd century AD
Newstead, Roxburghshire—a Roman fort
L   425mm

The tool is a solid bar of iron of rectangular cross-section which is bent at right angles at one end. The other end is socketed to hold a long wooden handle, which is here restored.

FRA 322

59 Iron fore-hammer

Late 1st century AD
Newstead, Roxburghshire—a Roman fort
L   300mm

This fore-hammer, suited to making spears and sword blades, has a cross-paned head and weighs 4lbs 1¼ozs. The shaft, which is here restored, would have been wedged into the central hole. Though this example is small, it would have been the smith's most basic type of hammer.

FRA 300
Curle 1911, 285, pl LXIII

60 Hammer tongs

Late 1st century AD
Newstead, Roxburghshire—a Roman fort
L   400mm

These hammer tongs were probably best suited to light work such as drawing out spearheads or forging bolts. It is interesting to note that they have been designed for left handed use—similar tongs are still used by modern blacksmiths.

FRA 229
Curle 1911, 286, pl LXIII; Sloane 1964, 91

61 Hoop tongs

Late 1st century AD
Newstead, Roxburghshire—a Roman fort
L   450mm

The tong's pincers project at right angles to the main body of the tool and this design suggests they were used for making and attaching the iron tyres which run round the circumference of wooden spoked wheels (see no 74–75). Similar tongs were used in later times by American pioneers. A very close parallel occurs at Silchester.

FRA 298
Curle 1911, 286, pl LXIII; Boon 1957, 185, fig 36.7; Sloane 1964, 91

62 Ingot

Late 1st century AD
Newstead, Roxburghshire—a Roman fort
L   295mm

In the Roman period all iron objects were wrought, not cast, as smiths did not have the necessary technology to create temperatures up to 1,540°C, the melting point of iron. However, they were able to reduce iron ore to metal at 1,100°C–1,150°C. Raw bloom is formed at this temperature and comes out of the furnace as a spongy lump encrusted with slag. The slag is removed with repeated reheating and heavy hammering. Individual blooms are sometimes welded together and hammered when red hot to

form blocks. This ingot represents a rare example of such a block of unused stock.

FRA 325
Curle 1911, 288, pl LXV

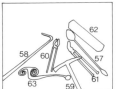

63 Ornamental bracket

Late 1st–2nd century AD
Newstead, Roxburghshire—a Roman fort
L   450mm

At one end of the bracket the bar is bent back to form a hoop and at the other is drawn out and turned to form spirals. Its use is uncertain though it has been suggested it forms the rail of a seat on a cart. It shows that the Roman blacksmith had the time and ability to produce ornamental metalwork along with the many utilitarian objects he made.

FRA 445
Curle 1913, 390–91, fig 2

64   Two-edged saw

Late 1st century AD
Newstead, Roxburghshire—a Roman fort
L   135mm

The blade of the small two-edged saw has both fine and coarse serrations, the upper row having two points per centimetre, and the lower three per centimetre. It is hafted in a split antler handle and held firm by two small metal rivets.

FRA 262
Curle 1911, 290, pl LXVIII

65   Auger

Late 1st century AD
Newstead, Roxburghshire—a Roman fort
L   287mm

A roughly octagonal bar of iron, terminating in a gouge at one end, and a triangular tang at the other, forms the auger. The tang would have been let into a wooden shaft which joined it to a 'T'-shaped cross-handle (the shaft is simulated in perspex). This provided a firm grip and adequate leverage for boring the large deep holes for which this tool was designed. Such spoon-bit augers are not uncommon among Roman tools but, like the 375mm long example from Brampton, Cumberland, this auger is unusually large, though it is dwarfed by some German examples.

FRA 256
Curle 1911, 280, pl LIX; Manning 1966, 15–16

66 Blades of planes

Late 1st–2nd century AD
Newstead, Roxburghshire—a Roman fort
L 145mm, 80mm

The larger of the two, known as a moulding plane, is designed to cut mouldings one inch wide. The iron plane blade would have been let into a tapering groove in a wooden stock—a design which was carried through into the Middle Ages. The second blade consists of two pieces of slightly curved iron welded together.

FRA 241, 242
Curle 1911, 281, pl LIX; Goodman 1964, 51; Salaman 1975, 338

67 Two-sided file

Late 1st century AD
Newstead, Roxburghshire—a Roman fort
L 294mm

The iron file is a slender leaf-shape, with a narrow tang of rectangular cross-section. The tang would normally be covered with a wooden handle, here simulated in perspex. The blade is of gently curving lozenge-shaped cross-section and has fine transverse teeth.

FRA 254
Curle 1911, 281, pl LIX

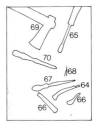

68 Compasses

Late 1st century AD
Newstead, Roxburghshire—a Roman fort
L   75mm

Unlike modern examples, this pair of iron compasses pivot at their point of intersection forming the shape of a St Andrew's Cross. This type, found in the ditch of the early fort, is also known from Pompeii, but otherwise is relatively rare.

FRA 323
Curle 1911, 309, pl LXXXII

69 Axe

Late 1st century AD
Newstead, Roxburghshire—a Roman fort
L   250mm

Manufactured from a solid piece of iron, this fine Roman axe bears a centurial mark and is inscribed in dots with the names BARRI and COMPITALICI. It weighs 6lbs and would have been hafted with a wooden handle, here restored, running parallel with the blade edge through the punched out eye. This is typically flanked by slight lugs.

FRA 236
Curle 1911, 282–83, pl LXI

70 Socketed chisel

Late 1st century AD
Newstead, Roxburghshire—a Roman fort
L   269mm

The main body of the tool is of rectangular cross-section but towards its flared cutting edge the blade thins. The socket is rounded above the shoulder of the chisel and part of the antler handle can still be seen in place. It seems to be a mortice chisel and the antler may have been used as a striking platform for a wooden mallet (see no 16). Similar examples were found at Silchester.

FRA 250
Curle 1911, 289, pl LIX; Boon 1957, 182, fig 35.3

THE STONEMASON

Masons building the Scott Monument, Edinburgh, about 1845.
From the calotype in the Scottish National Portrait Gallery.

71 Iron pick

Late 1st–2nd century AD
Newstead, Roxburghshire—a Roman fort
L   280mm

Although there is no evidence from Britain it seems likely that such picks would have been used with wedges in quarrying stone. The adze blade at the other end would have been used for some preliminary dressing of the blocks. The handle is restored.

FRA 234
Curle 1911, pl LVIII; Blagg 1976, 155

72 Iron adze

Late 1st–2nd century AD
Newstead, Roxburghshire—a Roman fort
L   330mm

This double adze would have been used to dress the stone prior to chiselling and smoothing. Sometimes this rough dressing was all that the stone received and the marks remain clearly visible. The handle is restored.

FRA 233
Curle 1911, pl LVIII; Blagg 1976, 157

E

73 Stone plumb-bob

2nd century AD
Mumrills, Stirlingshire—a Roman fort on
the Antonine Wall
H 78mm

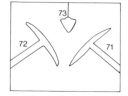

In form it is an inverted cone with a low circular
projection in the centre of the flat upper surface.
This projection is perforated to take the string,
which is here restored.

FRB 592
Macdonald & Curle 1929, 566, 565, fig 128

XV TRANSPORT

Keeping the army in provisions involved a complex supply
system made possible by excellent roads.

74 Wooden wheel

2nd century AD
Newstead, Roxburghshire—a Roman fort
D 1.14m

This wheel is reconstructed from fragments found at the bottom of pit LXX. The hub was carved from a single piece of wood. There were twelve spokes, of which five are modern restorations. All passed right through the felloe which is made of six pieces dowelled together. It is not clear whether the spokes projected beyond the felloe but the latter does not seem to have been made to take an iron tyre. The wheels from Newstead were probably used on carts or wagons, such an essential part of the Roman supply system, and there is no reason to believe that they were once part of chariots.

FRA 478
Curle 1911, 294

75 Iron tyre

Late 1st century AD
Inchtuthil, Perthshire—a Roman
legionary fortress
D 1.04m

Ten tyres for cart and wagon wheels were found to have been buried in exactly similar circumstances to the large hoard of nails (see no 18). The minor differences in the tyres suggest either that they were intended to fit a variety of wheels or that some of them were still in the process of manufacture. Since the pit in which they were buried was located in the east range of the *fabrica* or construction-shop the latter seems the more likely explanation. Immediately before fitting, the tyres would have been heated so that they expanded and could be easily fitted over the wooden wheels. They would then be rapidly cooled, using buckets of water, and the resulting shrinkage would ensure a tight fit on the wheel.

FY 183–91
J Rom Stud, 51, 1961, 160, 158–59, figs 9–10

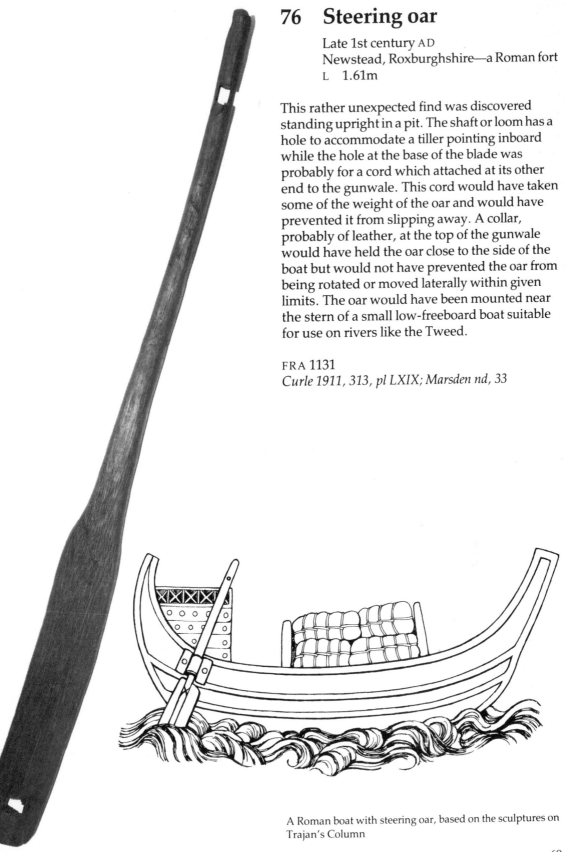

76 Steering oar

Late 1st century AD
Newstead, Roxburghshire—a Roman fort
L 1.61m

This rather unexpected find was discovered standing upright in a pit. The shaft or loom has a hole to accommodate a tiller pointing inboard while the hole at the base of the blade was probably for a cord which attached at its other end to the gunwale. This cord would have taken some of the weight of the oar and would have prevented it from slipping away. A collar, probably of leather, at the top of the gunwale would have held the oar close to the side of the boat but would not have prevented the oar from being rotated or moved laterally within given limits. The oar would have been mounted near the stern of a small low-freeboard boat suitable for use on rivers like the Tweed.

FRA 1131
Curle 1911, 313, pl LXIX; Marsden nd, 33

A Roman boat with steering oar, based on the sculptures on Trajan's Column

77 Saddle mounts

Late 1st century AD
Newstead, Roxburghshire—a Roman fort
L (of longest example) 200mm

Two sets of these curious bronze objects were
found at Newstead but not until recently has it
been possible to explain satisfactorily their use.
Among the rich leather finds from the Roman
fort at Valkenburg in Holland there were the
remains of a virtually complete leather saddle.
This saddle was designed to have two projections
at either end of the seat and the stiffening for
these projections would have been provided by
bronze mounts such as the Newstead pieces.
The outside of the mounts were themselves
covered with leather probably to enable them to
grip more effectively the leather of the saddle.
On one of the larger pieces there is scratched
XV SENECIO and below this, going in the reverse
direction, CRESCES. On each of the other three
pieces there is XII SENECIONIS. These
inscriptions probably identified the owner and
unit in which he was serving.

FRA 130
*Curle 1911, 177–78, pl XXXII; Groenman-van
Waateringe 1967, 106–21; MacMullen 1960, 35*

A reconstruction of the Roman saddle from
Valkenburg—after Groenman-van Waateringe

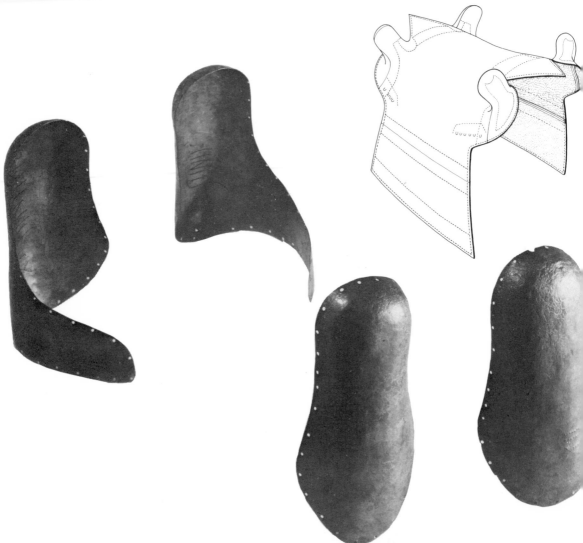

78 Iron head-stall

2nd century AD
Newstead, Roxburghshire—a Roman fort
W   114mm

This head-stall is plain except for the central disc.
Now much decayed, the disc was originally
decorated with concentric rings of millefiori
enamel with a brass edging.

FRA 495
Curle 1911, 297, pl LXXI; Taylor 1975

The head-stall in use—after Taylor

79   Harness-mounts

Late 1st century AD
Newstead, Roxburghshire—a Roman fort
H (of largest example)   65mm

Numerous examples of metal harness fittings,
many of them highly decorated, were found
during the excavations at Newstead. The three
examples here were intended to hang from
round discs or *phalerae* which were attached to
the leather straps of the harness. They are a
conventional representation of foliage with a
central pointed shoot flanked by leaves with
their points turned back. They are made of
bronze plated with silver which is now corroded
to give them a bluish tinge. A design of leaf and
tendril is tooled on the leaf-like surface and was
probably once filled with niello. Closely
comparable mounts have been found at the
Roman fort at Xanten in Germany.

FRA 525–27
Curle 1911, 300, pl LXXIII

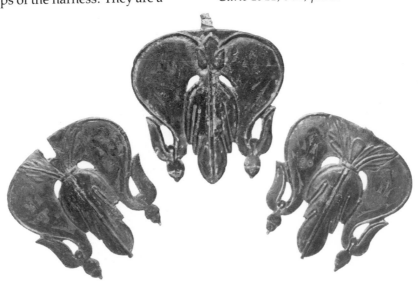

XVI RELIGION AND BURIAL

Tomb in Calton Cemetery, Edinburgh.

80 The goddess Brigantia

2nd or early 3rd century AD
Birrens, Dumfriesshire—a Roman fort
H   920mm

This relief provides a particularly good example
of a purely local, native goddess given oriental
and Roman trappings and rendered in the
plastic, three-dimensional manner that suits
these classical associations. She stands in the
front of a gabled niche, wearing a cloak and long
tunic with a gorgon's head on her breast and a
conical helmet surmounted by a crest and
encircled by a towered crown on her head. The
crown presumably represents the chief
Brigantian Roman city, York, while the breast
decoration is to be linked with Minerva, the
patron goddess of engineers, as is the spear in
her right hand and the shield standing to her left.
From her shoulders spring the wings of Victory
and in her left hand is a globe, presumably
indicating her power throughout the world. To
her right is standing an omphaloid stone of Juno
Caelistis or Regina, consort of Jupiter
Dolichenus. At the base of the relief there is a
short inscription:

BRIGANTIAE S(ACRVM): AMANDVS
ARC(H)ITECTVS EX IMPERIO IMP(ERATUM
FECIT)

which may be translated as 'Sacred to Brigantia:
Amandus, the engineer, fulfilled the order by
command'.

The Amandus of this inscription may be the
same man recorded on a building-inscription
found at Iversheim, near Bonn, Germany which
can be dated to AD 209. Since on this inscription
his rank is given as one grade higher than on that
from Iversheim it is usually assumed that this
relief must be dated to the 2nd or 3rd decade of
the 3rd century AD, when Amandus in his newly
promoted post was attached to the sixth Legion
based at York. Certainly, the amalgam of
attributes given to Brigantia accords well with
the cults most favoured in the Empire, in military
and court circles, during the early years of the
3rd century and this was a period when the cult
of Brigantia was officially encouraged. However,
the one major difficulty in accepting this dating is
that all the other evidence suggests that Birrens
was only occupied in the 2nd century. The
Brigantes were the major tribe in northern

England and their territory seems to have
extended into south-west Scotland.

FV 5
*Toynbee 1962, 157, pl 77; Collingwood & Wright
1965, 640–41, No 2901, pl XIX; Robertson 1975*

81 Altar

2nd century AD
Birrens, Dumfriesshire—a Roman fort
H   1.10m

The front of the altar is decorated with ivy leaves and rosettes and carries the following inscription:

MARTI ET VICTO
RIAE AVG(VSTI) C(IVES) RAE
TI MILIT(ANTES) IN COH(ORTE)
II TVNGR(ORVM) CVI
PRAEEST SILVIVS
AVSPEX PRAEF(ECTVS)
V(OTVM) S(OLVIT) L(IBENTES) M(ERITO)

This may be translated as follows—

'To Mars and the Emperor's Victory, the Raetian tribesmen serving in the Second Cohort of Tungrians under the command of Gaius Silvius Auspex, the prefect, willingly and deservedly fullfilled their vow'.

An altar from Birrens dedicated to Minerva by the same army unit under the same commander is now in Dumfries Museum. A detachment of the Second Cohort of Tungrians, which was raised in Belgium, served in the province of Raetia, in the eastern Alps, in the middle of the 2nd century. The soldiers who dedicated this altar would have been recruited at that time and returned with the cohort to Britain in the 150s AD, taking up residence at Birrens in 158.

FV 2
Collingwood & Wright 1965, 644, no 2100

82 Cremation urn and lid

2nd century AD
Newstead, Roxburghshire—a Roman fort
H   255mm

The urn shows no signs of having been specially made for the burial since it is a common enough form of jar. It was presumably selected from the fort's pottery store because it was the right size to contain the cremation. The jar has an everted rim and a broad band of lattice around the body. It was sealed with a round sandstone cover. The burial, one of two, was discovered in clearing out the ditch of the fort. Standing upright on a

sandstone slab, the urn was protected by four further slabs of sandstone placed so as to form a tent-like structure over it. Roman burials, either inhumations or cremations, are rare in Scotland.

FRA 1390
Curle 1911, 19, pl IV

83   Antler amulet

Late 1st century AD
Newstead, Roxburghshire—a Roman fort
D   70mm

It is a circular disc cut from the base of a red deer antler, the natural protuberances being left to form a frilled border. In the centre a phallic emblem has been carved in relief. Phallic emblems are commonly found on a large number of Roman objects and were considered to promote good luck and act as talismans against evil spirits. Despite this, close parallels for this amulet are rare in Britain, the best coming from Malton in Yorkshire, Dorchester in Dorset and Corbridge in Northumberland.

FRA 1172
Curle 1911, 314, pl LXXXIV; Corder 1948, 176, pl XXVIa; Green 1978, 58, pl 139

Appendix

The main sites represented
in the collections.

Excavations at the sites of the forts listed below have
produced substantial collections of material which form the
bulk of the National Museum's holdings. In addition, there
are small groups of finds from other sites together with
isolated discoveries. The inclusion of a site on this list,
however, does not mean that the National Museum holds all
the material from that site or, indeed, has material from every
excavation that has taken place on that site. The list is
designed to show the extent of our holdings of small finds
and does not take account of inscribed stones which are
adequately listed in Collingwood & Wright 1965.

Ardoch, Perthshire
    Christison, Cunningham, Anderson & Ross 1898
Birrens, Dumfriesshire
    Robertson 1975
Cadder, Lanarkshire
Camelon, Stirlingshire
    Christison, Buchanan & Anderson 1901
Cappuck, Roxburghshire
    Stevenson & Miller 1912
Cardean, Perthshire
Carpow, Perthshire
    Birley 1963
Castlecary, Stirlingshire
    Christison, Buchanan & Anderson 1903
Croy Hill, Dumbartonshire
    Macdonald 1932; Macdonald 1937
Fendoch, Perthshire
    Richmond & McIntyre 1939
Inchtuthil, Perthshire
    Abercromby, Ross & Anderson 1902
Lyne, Peeblesshire
    Christison & Anderson 1901; Steer & Feachem 1962
Mumrills, Stirlingshire
    Macdonald & Curle 1929; Steer 1961
Newstead, Roxburghshire
    Curle 1911; 1913; Richmond 1950
Oakwood, Selkirkshire
    Steer & Feachem 1952
Rough Castle, Stirlingshire
    Buchanan, Christison & Anderson 1905; Macdonald 1933

References

Abercromby, J, Ross, T & Anderson, J 1902 Account of
the excavation of the Roman station at Inchtuthil,
Perthshire, undertaken by the Society of Antiquaries of
Scotland in 1901, *Proc Soc Antiq Scot*, 36, 1901–02, 182–242.

Angus, N S, Brown, G T & Cleere, H F 1962 The iron nails
from the Roman legionary fortress at Inchtuthil,
Perthshire, *J Iron Steel Inst*, 200, 1962, 956–68.

Bagshawe, T W 1949 Romano-British hoes or rakes,
Antiq J, 29, 1949, 86–87.

Birley, R E 1963 Excavation of the Roman fortress at
Carpow, Perthshire, 1961–2, *Proc Soc Antiq Scot*, 96, 1962–63,
184–207.

Blagg, T F C 1976 Tools and techniques of the Roman
stonemason in Britain, *Britannia*, 7, 1976, 152–72.

Boon, G C 1957 *Roman Silchester, the archaeology of a
Romano-British town*. London, 1957.

Boon, G C 1966 Roman window glass from Wales, *J Glass
Stud*, 8, 1966, 41–45.

Buchanan, M, Christison, D & Anderson, J 1905 Report
on the Society's excavation of Rough Castle on the
Antonine Vallum, *Proc Soc Antiq Scot*, 39, 1904–05, 442–99.

Burley, E 1956 A catalogue and survey of the metal-work
from Traprain Law, *Proc Soc Antiq Scot*, 89, 1955–56,
118–226.

Christison, D & Anderson, J 1901 Excavation of the
Roman camp at Lyne, Peeblesshire, undertaken by the
Society of Antiquaries of Scotland in 1901, *Proc Soc Antiq
Scot*, 35, 1900–01, 154–86.

Christison, D, Buchanan, M & Anderson, J 1901 Account
of the excavation of the Roman station of Camelon, near
Falkirk, undertaken by the Society in 1900, *Proc Soc Antiq
Scot*, 35, 1900–01, 329–417.

Christison, D, Buchanan, M & Anderson, J 1903 Excavation
of Castlecary fort on the Antonine Vallum, *Proc Soc Antiq
Scot*, 37, 1902–03, 271–346.

Christison, D, Cunningham, J H, Anderson, J & Ross, T 1898
Account of the excavation of the Roman station at Ardoch,
Perthshire undertaken by the Society of Antiquaries of
Scotland in 1896–97, *Proc Soc Antiq Scot*, 32, 1897–98,
399–476.

Close-Brooks, J *forthcoming* A Roman iron flask from
Newstead, *Proc Soc Antiq Scot*, 109, 1977–78.

Collingwood, R G & Wright, R P 1965 *The Roman*

inscriptions of Britain. I Inscriptions on stone. Oxford, 1965.

Corder, P   1948   Miscellaneous small objects from the Roman fort at Malton, *Antiq J*, 28, 1948, 173–77.

Cree, J E & Curle, A O   1922   Account of the excavations on Traprain Law during the summer of 1921, *Proc Soc Antiq Scot*, 56, 1921–22, 189–260.

Cunnington, M E & Goddard, E H   1934   *Catalogue of the antiquities in the museum of the Wiltshire Archaeological and Natural Society at Devizes*, part II. Devizes, 1934.

Curle, J   1911   *A Roman frontier post and its people. The fort of Newstead in the parish of Melrose.* Glasgow, 1911.

Curle, J   1913   Notes on some undescribed objects from the Roman fort at Newstead, Melrose, *Proc Soc Antiq Scot*, 47, 1912–13, 384–405.

Curle, J   1932   An inventory of objects of Roman and provincial Roman origin found on sites in Scotland not definitely associated with Roman constructions, *Proc Soc Antiq Scot*, 66, 1931–32, 277–397.

Davies, J L   1977   Roman arrowheads from Dinorben and the Sagittarii of the Roman army, *Britannia*, 8, 1977, 257–70.

Davies, R W   1970   The Roman military medical service, *Saalburg Jhb*, 27, 1970, 84–104.

Dunbar, Mrs D   1930   Note on a Roman glass bottle from the parish of Turriff, about 1857, *Proc Soc Antiq Scot*, 64, 1929–30, 147–48.

Eggers, H J   1966   Römische Bronzefasse in Britannien, *Jhb Römisch-Germanischen Zentralmus Mainz*, 13, 1966, 67–164.

Frere, S   1972   *Verulamium excavations*, I. Oxford, 1972.
(=*Rep Res Comm Soc Antiq London*, 28)

Garbsch, J   1978   *Römische Paraderustungen.* München, 1978.

Gillam, J P   1957   Types of Roman coarse pottery vessels in northern Britain, *Archaeol Aeliana*, 4 Ser, 35, 1957, 180–215.

Goodman, W L   1964   *The history of woodworking tools.* London, 1964.

Green, M J   1976   *The religions of civilian Roman Britain.* Oxford, 1976.
(=*Brit Archaeol Rep*, 24).

Green, M J   1978   *Small cult-objects from the military areas of Roman Britain.* Oxford, 1978.
(=*Brit Archaeol Rep*, 52).

Groenman-van Waateringe, W   1967   *Romeins Lederwerk uit Valkenburg Z H.* Groningen, 1967.
(=*Nederlandse Oudheden*, 2).

Haevernick, T E & Hahn-Weinheimer, P   1955   Untersuchungen römischer Fensterglaser, *Saalburg Jhb*, 14, 1955, 65–73.

Harden, D B   1961   Domestic window glass, Roman, Saxon and Medieval in E M Jope (ed), *Studies in building history*, London, 1961, 39–63.

Hartley, B R   1969   Samian ware or *terra sigillata* in R G Collingwood & I A Richmond, *The archaeology of Roman Britain*, 2 ed, London, 1969, 235–51.

Henig, M   1970   A Roman intaglio, *Burlington Mag*, 112(806), 1970, 307.

Henshall, A S   1952   Early textiles found in Scotland: part 1 (locally made), *Proc Soc Antiq Scot*, 86, 1951–52, 1–29.

Isings, C   1957   *Roman glass from dated finds.* Groningen/Djakarta, 1957.
(=*Archaeol Traiectina*, 2).

Liversidge, J   1955   *Furniture in Roman Britain.* London, 1955.

Macdonald, Sir G   1932   Notes on the Roman forts at Old Kilpatrick and Croy Hill, and a relief of Jupiter Dolichenus, *Proc Soc Antiq Scot*, 66, 1931–32, 219–76.

Macdonald, Sir G   1933   Notes on the Roman forts at Rough Castle and Westerwood, with a postscript, *Proc Soc Antiq Scot*, 67, 1932–33, 243–96.

Macdonald, Sir G   1934a   *The Roman Wall in Scotland*, 2 ed, Oxford, 1934.

Macdonald, Sir G   1934b   Roman coins found in Scotland (III), including a hoard from Falkirk, *Proc Soc Antiq Scot*, 68, 1933–34, 27–40.

Macdonald, Sir G   1934c   A hoard of Roman denarii from Scotland, *Numis Chron*, 5 ser, 14, 1934, 1–30.

Macdonald, Sir G   1937   A further note on the Roman fort at Croy Hill, *Proc Soc Antiq Scot*, 71, 1936–37, 32–71.

Macdonald, Sir G & Curle, A O   1929   The Roman fort at Mumrills, near Falkirk, *Proc Soc Antiq Scot*, 63, 1928–29, 396–575.

MacMullen, R   1960   Inscriptions on armor and the supply of arms in the Roman Empire, *Amer J Archaeol*, 64, 1960, 23–40.

MacGregor, M   1976   *Early Celtic art in north Britain. A study of decorative metalwork from the third century BC to the third century AD.* Leicester, 1976.

Manning, W H   1966   A hoard of Romano-British ironwork from Brampton, Cumberland, *Trans Cumberland Westmorland Antiq Archaeol Soc*, 66, 1966, 1–36.

Manning, W H   1970   Mattocks, hoes, spades and related tools in Roman Britain in A Gailey & A Fenton (eds), *The spade in northern and Atlantic Europe*, Belfast, 1970, 18–29.

Manning, W H   1976   *A catalogue of Romano-British ironwork in the Museum of Antiquities, Newcastle upon Tyne.* Newcastle, 1976.

Marsden, P R V   nd   *A ship of the Roman period, from Blackfriars, in the City of London.* London, nd.

McIntyre, J & Richmond, I A   1934   Tents of the Roman army and leather from Birdoswald, *Trans Cumberland Westmorland Antiq Archaeol Soc*, 34, 1934, 62–90.

Moore, C N   1978   An enamelled bronze skillet-handle from Brough—on—Fosse and the distribution of similar vessels, *Britannia*, 9, 1978, 319–27.

Phillips, E J   1974   The Roman distance slab from Bridgeness, *Proc Soc Antiq Scot*, 105, 1972–74, 176–82.

Piggott, S   1953   Three metal-work hoards of the Roman period from southern Scotland, *Proc Soc Antiq Scot*, 87, 1952–53, 1–50.

Pitt Rivers, A H L   1892   *Excavations in Cranborne Chase*, III. Privately printed.

Richmond, I A   1950   Excavations at the Roman fort of Newstead, 1947, *Proc Soc Antiq Scot*, 84, 1949–50, 1–38.

Richmond, I A & McIntyre, J   1939   The Agricolan fort at Fendoch, *Proc Soc Antiq Scot*, 73, 1938–39, 110–54.

Robertson, A S   1975   *Birrens (Blatobulgium).* Edinburgh, 1975.

Robertson, A, Scott, M & Keppie, L   1975   *Bar Hill: a Roman fort and its finds.* Oxford, 1975.
(=*Brit Archaeol Rep*, 16).

Robinson, H R   1975   *The armour of Imperial Rome.* London, 1975.

Salaman, R A   1975   *Dictionary of tools.* London, 1975.

Sherlock, D   1976   Roman folding spoons *Trans London Middlesex Archaeol Soc*, 27, 1976, 250–55.